THE
ALLIGATOR

BY
SUSAN DUDLEY MORRISON

EDITED BY
DR. HOWARD SCHROEDER

**Professor in Reading and Language Arts
Dept. of Elementary Education
Mankato State University**

PRODUCED AND DESIGNED BY
BAKER STREET PRODUCTIONS
Mankato, MN

CRESTWOOD HOUSE
Mankato, Minnesota

CIP

LIBRARY OF CONGRESS CATALOGING IN PUBLICATION DATA

Morrison, Susan Dudley.
   The alligator.

   Bibliography: p.
   Includes index.
   SUMMARY: Discusses the physical characteristics, habits, and behavior of alligators.
   1. Alligators--Juvenile literature. (1. Alligators) I. Schroeder, Howard. II. Baker Street Productions. III. Title.
QL666.C925M67   1984   597.98   83-21034
ISBN 0-89686-242-9 (lib. bdg.)

International Standard Book Number:	Library of Congress Catalog Card Number:
Library Binding 0-89686-242-9	83-21034

ILLUSTRATION CREDITS:

Lynn Rogers: Cover
Nadine Orabona: 4, 8, 41
Pat Toops: 7, 29
Connie Toops: 10, 13, 16, 19, 20, 23, 26-27, 31, 36, 39, 44
Brian Parker/Tom Stack & Associates: 15, 35
David Meardon: 32

CRESTWOOD HOUSE

Hwy. 66 South, Box 3427
Mankato, MN 56002-3427

Introduction **4**
Chapter I **6**
   Age of reptiles
   Crocodilians today
Chapter II **10**
   Plates, flaps, and eyeshine
   Powerful jaws and teeth
   How big are they?
   Crocodiles are different
Chapter III **17**
   Life in the swamp
   Home for the winter
Chapter IV **22**
   Finding a mate
   Building a nest
   Threats to the eggs
   Life in the egg
   The hatchlings are born
   Growing up
Chapter V **33**
   Mammals, fish, birds & reptiles
   Attacks on humans
Chapter VI **36**
   Handbags and hunters
   An endangered species
   Too many alligators?
   Farms and ranches
   Looking for answers
   What's in the future
Map **45**
Index/Glossary **46**

Alligators have long had a bad reputation. Their scales and long tail have made people think of dragons. People have been afraid of their big mouth and sharp teeth. Alligators have been called monsters. Their eyes glow red when a light shines on them in the dark.

The alligator's name comes from the Spanish words, *el lagarto,* meaning the lizard. Many people call the animal a " 'gator." That is the alligator's nickname.

Alligators may look scary, but they really aren't as fierce as people have believed. They attack very few humans. Usually they are shy and keep away from

With their big mouths and sharp teeth, alligators seem like monsters from the deep!

people if they can. Sometimes, though, an alligator will eat a pet dog which strays within its range.

On the other hand, people have killed millions of alligators through the years. Even before European explorers came to North America, Native Americans killed alligators. They used alligator hides to cover drums. When the Europeans arrived, they killed alligators for sport, and because they were afraid of them.

Hunting for alligators in the United States had become a big business by the late 1800's. Skin taken from the alligator's belly could be made into leather. The leather was used to make handbags, luggage, and shoes.

By 1900, hunters had killed more than two-and-a-half million alligators in Florida. In Louisiana and other states, millions more were killed.

So many alligators were killed, that some people believed there would soon be no more alligators left in the United States. They wanted to save the alligator. They wanted their children and grandchildren to be able to see it. In 1944, Florida became the first state to pass a law to protect the alligator. Other states where alligators lived also passed laws like the Florida law.

The new laws worked. Today, more than two million alligators live in the southern United States. Some areas have so many alligators that the states are once again allowing them to be hunted.

CHAPTER ONE:

Age of reptiles

Alligators are part of a family that has been around for several thousand years. They are part of a group of animals called crocodilians. The first crocodilians appeared during the Mesozoic Era. The Mesozoic Era is also called the Age of Reptiles.

During the Age of Reptiles, these animals thrived. All types of crocodilians roamed the world. Some were only a foot (31 cm) long. Others were giants, up to fifty feet (15.2 m) long.

Near the end of the Age of Reptiles, the earth began to change. The weather became colder and drier. Plains and deserts appeared where swamps had once been.

As the reptiles homes dried up and their food disappeared, many of the them died. The dinosaurs were among the first to go. Next, the giant crocodilians, which fed on the dinosaurs, disappeared.

The smaller crocodilians survived because they lived in areas that still had a good supply of water. Their homes were in swamps, lakes, and rivers in the warmer parts of the world.

Crocodilians today

Today, only three types of crocodilians exist: crocodiles, gharials, and alligators. There are sixteen types of crocodiles. They live only in areas of the world where the weather is quite warm. These areas are called the tropics. The only crocodiles in the United States — except for those in zoos — live in the southwestern part of Florida. They cannot live in areas farther north.

An adult alligator suns itself.

The gharial is a small reptile. It looks like a lizard and is found in India.

Alligators are part of a group of animals called *alligatoridae.* There are two kinds of alligators. The Chinese alligator is found in the eastern part of China. It is smaller than the American alligator. The more common American alligator lives in the south-eastern United States. It has not been found in any other country.

Most American alligators live in Florida and Louisiana. Others inhabit the swamps and rivers of Georgia, parts of Texas, southern Alabama, southern Arkansas, and the coastal plains of South Caro-

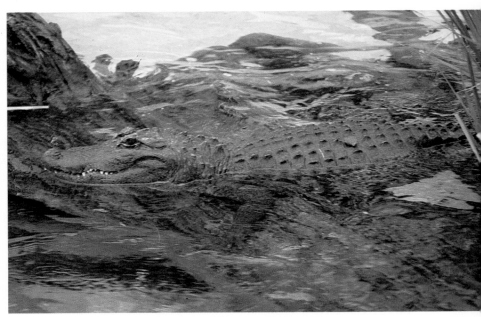

This adult "gator" was photographed in Mississippi.

lina and southern North Carolina. Some also live along the southeastern tip of Oklahoma, and north up the Mississippi Valley to eastern Arkansas and northwestern Mississippi. The alligator is the only crocodilian which lives outside the tropics. It can stand colder weather than other crocodilians.

Scientists call the American alligator the *alligator mississipiensis.* That's because some of the first alligators spotted by scientists were found along the banks of the Mississippi River.

Alligators, like other reptiles, have traits which set them apart from mammals like man. People keep the inside of their bodies at a steady temperature. Whether it is cold or hot outside, people stay the same temperature inside. We sweat to cool our bodies in summer. We wrap up in warm clothes in winter. Alligators cannot do that. Their bodies are the same temperature as their surroundings. That is why they can't be in places where it gets very hot or very cold. When it is sunny and hot, they stay in the shade or in the water. When it is cool, they sit in the sun.

Some people have bought baby alligators and taken them home as pets. When the pets got too big, some owners flushed them down their toilets. Because of this, it's been said that alligators live in the sewers of New York. They couldn't really live there, however. New York's winter weather is much too cold for alligators.

CHAPTER TWO:

Plates, flaps, and eyeshine

It is strange that people will pay high prices for things made of alligator hides and still think of the alligator itself as being ugly.

The alligator looks like an old log floating on the

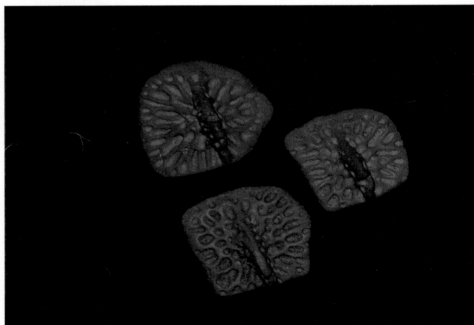

This photograph shows some of the "plates" that make up the skin on the back of an alligator.

water. Its skin is scaly and covered with bumps. Bony plates protect its neck, back, and tail. Its snout is broad and flat.

On top of the snout, at its tip, are the animal's nostrils. This lets, the alligator breathe with just its snout above water. When the alligator dives under the water, its nostrils close to prevent water from coming in. Its ears, high on the head, are also protected from the water. A thin flap of skin covers them.

Upper and lower eyelids protect the alligator's eyes. It also has a third eyelid, which protects its eyes when it swims underwater. The alligator can see through this eyelid. It's like wearing a pair of goggles.

The alligator's eyes have another strange feature. Light enters the eyes, as it does in all animals. In other animals, however, most of the light is reflected back out. In the alligator, the light is reflected back into the eyes. This helps the alligator see better at night. It also causes the alligator's eyes to glow in the dark when a light shines on them. This is called eyeshine. Years ago, hunters learned that they could spot alligators at night by shining flashlights on the water where they lived. Many of the animals were tracked down and killed that way.

Some alligators learned to avoid the hunters. As soon as a light was put on them, they dove under the water. These alligators were called "blinkers."

Powerful jaws and teeth

The alligator's huge mouth is filled with teeth. An adult alligator may have up to eighty teeth, divided between the upper and lower parts of its jaw. The alligator doesn't chew its prey, though. The teeth are used to rip and tear the animal which will be the alligator's dinner. The alligator swallows the animal in pieces.

The fourth tooth in the lower jaw and the ninth tooth in the upper jaw on either side of the alligator's mouth are the largest. In the biggest alligators, these teeth can be three or more inches (8 cm) long. Alligators are always growing new teeth. The new teeth grow inside the old teeth. An alligator's tooth lasts about one year. When the old tooth wears out, a new one takes its place. When an alligator gets old, it stops growing new teeth. Some old alligators have very few teeth left in their mouths.

The alligator's lower jaw opens and shuts just as a human's does. The upper jaw does not move up and down. Scientists think the animal's taste buds are on the outside of its jaws. When looking for food, the alligator moves its head from side to side. When the side of its jaw touches something, the tastes buds tell it whether the object is good to eat. If it is, the alligator snaps it up and swallows it.

The alligator's jaws are so powerful they can snap off a human's leg. However, a person can hold an alligator's jaws shut with their hands. That is because the muscles that close the jaw are much stronger than the muscles that open it.

Alligators have four legs and webbed feet. The front legs are shorter than the back legs. Some scientists believe this shows that the alligator's ancestors walked upright, the way people do.

Each front foot has five toes, with sharp claws. The two outer toes are smaller than the rest. The

The hind foot of an alligator has only four toes.

back feet have four toes and a stump of bone, instead of a fifth toe.

The alligator has intestines, but no bladder. The urine flows directly from the kidney, through a duct, and out a vent. The vent, or hole, is near the base of the alligator's tail, on the underside. All the wastes from the alligator's body go out through the vent.

How big are they?

When baby alligators are born, they are about eight-and-a-half inches (22 cm) long. They grow as much as a foot (31 cm) a year. Males grow larger than females. The largest females are rarely over nine feet (2.7 m) long. It is quite rare to see an alligator longer than twelve feet (3.7 m) in the wild. Most of the largest ones have been killed for their hides. Today, the biggest alligators are usually in zoos. The Gatorland Zoo in Kissimmee, Florida has one alligator that is fifteen feet (4.6 m) long. The largest male alligator ever recorded was just over nineteen feet (5.8 m) long.

Alligators seem to grow quite steadily until they are about eight years old. Then they grow more slowly for several more years. It is believed the oldest alligators live to be about fifty years old. Females may not live to be as old as males.

An alligator that has algae growing on its body might be sick.

Sometimes an alligator will have something that looks like moss growing on its back. This does not mean the alligator is old. The moss is really algae. The algae is a type of plant that grows in moist and warm places. It will grow on an alligator which is sick or not properly cared for at a zoo. An alligator covered with too much algae will probably die.

Crocodiles are different

When the explorers from Europe first saw alligators in the New World, they mixed them up with the fierce crocodiles of the African tropics. However, crocodiles and alligators are different in several ways. The most obvious is their snouts. Alligators' snouts are rounder than the pointed snout of the crocodile. When alligators shut their jaws, their teeth often can't be seen. A crocodile's teeth often stick out over the closed jaw. Alligators also aren't as fierce as the "man-eating" crocodile. Most times alligators will ignore people, or try to escape, when they see them coming.

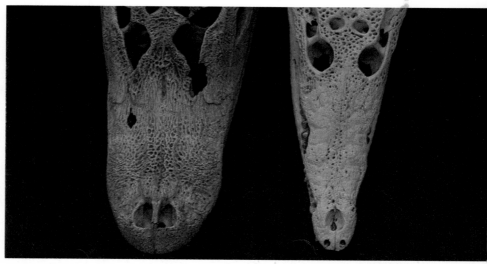

This photograph of the skulls of an alligator (left) and a crocodile (right) shows the difference in their snouts. The alligator's snout is rounder.

CHAPTER THREE:

Life in the swamp

Spanish moss hangs down from the cypress trees like a fine mist in a swamp. Peat, formed from rotted plants centuries old, covers the ground. In some places the peat is twenty feet (6.1 m) deep. The ground squishes when someone walks on it. The Indians named one such swamp Okefenokee, which means "land of the trembling earth." The swamp is still called by that name today. It covers 412,000 acres of land in Georgia. Most of the swamp lies in the Okefenokee National Wildlife Refuge. Animals are protected there. Deep in the swamp, where purple pickerelweed and yellow and white water lilies grow, thousands of alligators live.

Besides swamps, alligators live in rivers, streams, ponds, lakes, and marshes. In Florida, alligators can also be found living in culverts that drain water under roads running through marshes.

The area where alligators live is called their habitat. Wherever the alligator chooses to live, it must be warm. It must also be close to water. Alligators prefer fresh water. They don't like water that is too muddy or too salty. They like shallow water, not over twenty (6.1 m) feet deep. An alligator swims in the water, hunts for food there, mates, and cools off on hot summer days. Where water is cool, alligators can be seen lying with their bellies in the water and their backs to the sun. That way, they can keep their bodies the right temperature, not too hot or too cold. Alligators don't bask in the sun all day. They would get too hot. Often they lie under the shade of trees or the giant leaves of plants.

A favorite alligator spot is the Everglades. This freshwater marsh fills about five thousand square miles (12,950 sq. km) in southern Florida. The Everglades National Park, within the marsh, was set up in 1934. The park is set aside for animals and plants to grow, and for people to enjoy.

Islands dot the wet marsh. Some are no larger than a clump of trees. Others may stretch for miles. A jungle of plants and trees grow on the islands. Between the islands run channels of water, where water lilies and cypress trees grow. Saw grass, its sharp spikes aimed at the sky, covers much of the area.

The Everglades teems with all kinds of animal life. Fish and birds by the thousands live here. They feed on the many kinds of mosquitoes and other insects found in the marsh. A rare puma, Florida's panther, may be lurking nearby. Smaller animals live in the Everglades, too. They make tasty dining for the alligators which thrive here.

Home for
the winter

In the winter, some marshes and swamps dry up, leaving only small areas with water. In the marshy land of the Everglades, alligators dig themselves large holes or basins. There they stay for the winter.

"Gator holes" can be quite large and deep.

The holes can be as deep as twelve feet (3.7 m) and several yards (meters) wide. These "gator holes" fill with water. The water in the holes is warmer than the air. It helps protect the alligator from the winter's cold. Winter usually lasts from mid-November to mid-March.

To dig its hole, an alligator burrows down into the soft earth with its nose. Using its sides, it heaps the mushy plants, roots, and dirt around the edges of the hole. An alligator may also reuse a hole dug the winter before. Sometimes, an alligator will use a

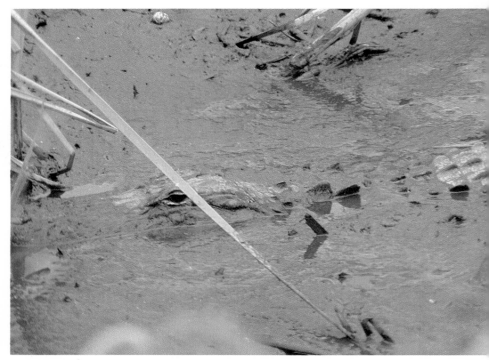

This alligator soaks itself in a small, muddy hole.

natural depression, or hollow, in the marsh as its winter home.

It is easy to spot a gator hole. Willow trees and other plants grow in the rich dirt piled around the hole. Like a good housekeeper, the alligator keeps its home clean. It bites off any plants that begin to grow in the hole.

During the dry season, the grasses in the marsh become brittle. The canals and streams dry up and often the gator holes are the only source of water for miles around. All kinds of creatures seek out the gator hole for its life-giving water. Deer come to take a sip. Frogs, fish, and turtles swim in the water. Insects and tiny animals crowd around, and birds pause for a drink. Each adult alligator has its own gator hole, but young alligators are allowed to share the winter home with their elders.

You might think that the alligator would have quite a feast eating all the animals gathered at its hole. But alligators eat very little in the winter, because they don't move around much. The cold slows them down. For about four months, they rest and wait for spring.

An alligator living on a river uses its nose to dig out a space in the river bank. In areas where the land is often flooded, an alligator may dig into the water-soaked ground for its winter home. Alligators living in lakes which do not dry up don't seem to need to dig a special home for the winter.

CHAPTER FOUR:

Finding a mate

When spring comes, alligators climb out of their winter homes to greet the warmth. They soon begin their search for mates. Both males and females call to each other in a strange bellowing roar. The loud bellow is made by air which is forced out of the alligator's mouth and throat. One alligator expert said it sounds something like a loud chainsaw. Alligators bellow at other times of the year, too. Most scientists agree, though, that alligators bellow in the spring to help them find mates.

In April or May, the alligators mate. They are five years old, or older, when they mate. Mating is done in the water. The male and female swim quickly around in a circle. The male often lies beside the female in the water. He follows her wherever she goes. The male pats the female's back and sides with his front legs. He blows bubbles in the water near her. Sometimes the mating game can last longer than two weeks.

At last, the male alligator swims on top of the female. Once the male has fertilized the eggs inside the female, he swims away. A baby alligator will grow inside each fertilized egg.

Building a nest

The female alligator must now begin her motherly duties. A few weeks after mating, she builds her nest. Most often, she builds the nest about ten to fifteen feet (3.0-4.6 m) from the water. The female alligator will search until she finds a spot in the shade. Sometimes she picks a spot under a cypress tree. In other areas, large leaves of plants shade the nest from the sun.

The female alligator builds her nest using grasses and plants that are nearby.

The female alligator uses her hind feet and sides to pile up grasses and plants for the nest. She uses whatever is nearby to build it. Sometimes the nest will be partly made of sand. If it is near salt water, it may have sea shells in it. In the Everglades, blades of saw grass are used.

If the female alligator does not like the first nest, she will leave it and start a new one. Often, she will build two or three nests before she is satisfied.

Shaped like a cone, the nest stands two to two-and-one-half feet (62-77 cm) high. The female alligator sits on top of the nest to pack it down. She may spend two to three days building the nest. The large mound is between four and six feet (1.2-1.8 m) across at the bottom. Once the mound is in place, she digs out the center of the nest with her hind feet. The hole is about one foot deep and nine inches across. There, she will lay her eggs.

The eggs are laid three weeks after the alligators have mated, usually in late May or early June. The mother stands over the hole she has made at the top of the nest. As the eggs are laid, she holds a foot under them. That breaks their fall and stops them from cracking. A female alligator can lay up to sixty eggs at one time. The average female, however, lays about thirty-five eggs.

Once the eggs are inside the nest, the female covers them with plants. The plants, as they decay, give off heat. This helps keep the eggs warm during the night.

24

But the eggs must not get too hot, either, or they will not hatch. During the day, the mother travels back and forth between the nest and the water nearby. Soaking wet, she lies on the nest. This helps cool the nest and keeps it from drying out. As the mother travels back and forth between the nest and the water nearby, she wears a path. These paths are known as "alligator roads." Males make them, too, as they come and go from their favorite areas.

Threats to the eggs

It will take about nine weeks for the eggs to hatch. During that time, the mother alligator will usually stay near the nest. Most mother alligators will guard the eggs if they see an animal or a person get too close to the nest. She will open her mouth and hiss. Sometimes she will walk toward the intruder to scare it away.

Some mothers hide when people come near her nest. Scientists seem to think that they may be afraid of being shot.

The worst enemies, of the unborn alligator growing inside the eggs, are predators and water.

Predators will eat the eggs. Raccoons like to eat alligator eggs. If they find a nest that isn't guarded, they will have a feast. The next day, the hungry

During the day, the female travels between her nest and water. Her wet body keeps the nest cool and moist.

raccoon will come back for another meal of eggs. Each day, it will return until the eggs are all gone. Wild hogs also like alligator eggs.

The eggs may also be destroyed if water floods the nest. This often happens when the water level rises after the eggs have been laid. Sometimes the water rises too high in the marsh because people have built dams and canals to stop the water from flooding their homes and land. This floods the nest.

During dry spells, people often will use the water in the marsh for their farms and gardens. This can dry out the nests and the land around them. It will also prevent the alligator eggs from hatching.

Life in the egg

Inside the egg, the unborn alligator is curled up, its head doubled over its body. The shell is thin enough to let air in so the alligator can breathe. The egg is white and shiny and about three inches (8 cm) long.

The unborn alligator has quite a cozy home inside the egg. A tube connected to the baby brings food from the egg yolk. The egg white also provides the unborn alligator with food and water. Another layer of the egg stores the wastes from the baby alligator.

Protecting the inner egg is a tough layer of skin called a membrane. The membrane helps keep the baby alive, even if the eggshell is cracked. Fluid surrounds the baby and protects it.

As the alligator grows bigger inside the egg, the shell begins to crack. The baby alligator has a small, sharp bump on the end of its snout. This is called an egg tooth. The baby alligator uses the egg tooth to chip its way out of the membrane inside the eggshell.

The hatchlings are born

Right before the baby is ready to hatch, it will cry out. The cry sounds like a grunt. If the mother is

Only baby alligators have stripes.

nearby, she will hear the baby cry. Some scientists report that the mother alligator will uncover the nest with her mouth so the babies can get out. The baby alligator crawls out of the egg head first. If the mother is not around, the baby alligators will crawl out of the nest themselves.

The baby alligators, called hatchlings, are only about eight-and-a-half inches (22 cm) long. They have black sides and backs, with white stripes. The belly is white. The white stripes turn yellow soon after the alligator hatches. As an adult, the alligator will lose these stripes.

As soon as the hatchlings are out of the nest, they head for water. They are born knowing they must go there. If they are near a gator hole, they may head for that.

Once in the water, the hatchlings eat minnows, small crayfish, and other small water animals. The hatchlings must be very careful or they will get eaten by predators. The great blue heron and other birds are ready to pounce on the hatchlings. So are snakes, large fish, turtles, and bullfrogs. Scientists have even found hatchlings — and eggs — inside the stomachs of adult alligators.

The cry of a hatchling will most often bring an adult running to the rescue. Even adults, which are not the parents, will come when called by a hatchling. Even so, scientists think only about ten percent of the hatchlings live beyond the first year.

A mother alligator gives her babies a ride.

Growing up

Once young alligators reach four years old, they are considered adults and are no longer welcome in another adult's area. The adult alligator does not want other adults to bother it. When another adult comes too near, the alligator will open its mouth and hiss.

Young adults have to move through the marsh or swamp in search of new homes. They leave trails behind them as they crawl over the marsh grass. These alligator roads are used year after year by alligators on the move.

Alligators travel quickly on land and in the water. They can swim about six miles per hour, as fast as a small electric motor boat. On land, they lunge forward or slip down the side of a river bank into the water to escape enemies. They cannot outrun a race horse, as some people think. But they can run as fast as a human.

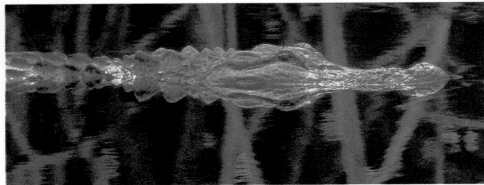

Alligators can swim six miles per hour.

CHAPTER FIVE:

Mammals, fish, birds & reptiles

Adult alligators often feed on the same animals that eat hatchlings. Snakes, frogs, birds, and fishes make a good meal. The alligator's strong jaws can crack open a turtle's shell with no trouble. A nonpoisonous snake will be snapped up and swallowed.

An alligator is more careful when eating a poisonous snake. It grabs the snake in its mouth and shakes it until it is dead. Then the alligator eats the snake. That way, the snake cannot bite the alligator in the eye, a soft spot where the poison could enter the body. If the snake is too big for one meal, the alligator will save it for later. It holds the remains in its mouth until it is hungry again.

Alligators living near the sea may eat shrimp, crabs, and fish. Mammals may also be on the menu. Alligators eat rats, mice, muskrats, rabbits, mink, pigs, and dogs. The largest alligators have been known to attack cattle and large game animals, like deer.

If an alligator's stomach were cut open, many insects might be found inside. The insects most likely were eaten by the alligator's prey — frogs, birds, and snakes. The adult alligator probably does not eat insects itself.

Alligators may swallow plants while they are eating. However, they cannot digest them. Meat is the alligator's only food. Because the alligator is a reptile, it does not eat as much as a human does. People have to eat often. Their food helps create energy to keep them warm. A reptile doesn't have to heat its body from the inside. It relies only on the sun to keep warm. At Gatorland Zoo in Florida, adult alligators are fed only once a week.

Sometimes alligators will swallow rocks or pieces of wood. Scientists believe these may be used to help the alligator grind up food in its stomach. These hard objects are called gastroliths.

Attacks on humans

Though alligators have been known to kill a human, it is very rare. Many times each year people come in contact with alligators in Florida. Yet only about five attacks a year occur there. Since 1970, three people have been killed in Florida by alligators.

When alligators were hunted they were afraid of people. They hid when they saw people coming. With laws now banning hunting in effect, some alligators are no longer afraid of humans. However, alligators usually avoid attacking something bigger than they are. A man or woman, standing up, looks too big to attack. Most alligator attacks have been on children or on adults who were swimming, sitting, or kneeling by a river or lake.

Alligators survive quite well in lakes and ponds near areas where people live. Some become quite used to people. Sometimes people feed them. Then the alligators come to expect food from humans. Some alligator experts worry that a small child may fall into a pond where an alligator lives. The alligator, expecting food, may attack. That is why it is against the law in Florida to hand-feed alligators.

Feeding alligators is against the law in Florida.

CHAPTER SIX:

Handbags
and hunters

People have always been much more of a threat to alligators than alligators to people. The hides, with their evenly placed scales, make fine leather. The

This photograph shows the hide from the belly of an alligator, and a shoe that was made from a hide.

leather can be used for shoes, handbags, luggage, and other goods.

Once hunters found out years ago that people would pay high prices for items made from alligator hides, they killed millions of them. Usually two hunters would go out into the swamp or marsh in a boat at night. One would shine a light in the alligators' eyes. The other would shoot the alligators in the head. Sometimes, a hunter would pull the alligators out of the water with a sharp hook attached to a long pole. Then the hunter would kill the alligator with an ax. Between 1930 and 1940, more than one million alligators were killed in Florida alone.

Starting in the 1940's, people began to fear all the alligators in the country would be killed. States where alligators lived began to pass laws to protect them. The laws let hunters kill alligators only during certain times of the year. Some people ignored the laws. They killed alligators whenever they could and sold their hides. These people, called poachers, were paid a lot of money for the alligator. There weren't enough wardens to patrol all the lands where the alligators lived and the killing continued.

By the late 1950's, people saw that the laws weren't tough enough to save the alligator. New laws were passed. In 1964, Louisiana banned the killing of all alligators. Other states passed their own laws to protect the alligator.

An endangered species

In 1967, the United States declared the alligator an "endangered species." That meant it was in danger of being wiped out forever. Because it was an endangered species, the alligator had to be protected by laws in each state where it lived. As the laws were passed, alligator hides became harder to get. Poachers got even more money for the ones they were able to bring to the buyers. People still paid a lot of money for things made out of alligator hides.

The shipping of alligator hides between states was banned. People weren't allowed to ship them to other countries, either. In some areas, goods made of alligator hides could not be sold. The sale of alligator meat was also not allowed.

The campaign to save the alligator began to work. Most of the poachers stopped killing alligators. It was very hard for them to find someone to buy the hides because of the new laws. The guns lay silent. More and more alligators began to appear in the swamps and marshes. Lakes and ponds near houses soon had their own alligators in them.

In 1975, the United States took alligators off the endangered species list. Alligators are now classified as "threatened" in some areas. That means they still need some protection, but states may let hunters kill

The hide on the left has been "tanned," or treated to preserve it; the hide on the right is untanned.

a certain number. It is also legal now to sell things made from alligator hides.

Too many alligators?

There are so many alligators in some southern states, they are becoming pests. Most people are afraid of alligators, especially the big ones. They don't want them in their ponds and lakes. The alligators don't often harm their human neighbors. Sometimes, though, they eat pet dogs. New laws are now being made to help control the alligators.

In Florida, the state government hires hunters to kill alligators which are bothering people. These are called "nuisance alligators." Once the alligator has been killed, the state sells the hide at an auction. The buyers come from the United States and Europe. Most of the world's leather makers, or tanners, of alligator hide are in Europe.

The state of Florida also sells the meat from the alligators. Restaurants buy it and serve it. Often the meat is deep fried. It looks like pork, with a mild seafood flavor. Some people think alligator meat is very good. About eighty to one hundred pounds (36.4-45.5 kg) of meat comes from a ten-foot, (3 m) five hundred pound (227.3 kg) alligator. People used

Some areas now have so many alligators that hunters are hired to kill a certain number of them.

to think just the tail meat was good to eat. Now, meat from the whole body is eaten.

The state of Florida gets some of the money from the sale of dead alligators. A hunter hired by the state gets the rest of the money. In 1982, about 2,100 nuisance alligators were killed in Florida.

Florida also let hunters kill four hundred alligators in three lakes in the north-central part of the state in 1982. The hunt was held to lower the number of alligators in the area. The state sold the hides for the hunters and gave them a share of the money.

In Louisiana, hunters were allowed to kill between fifteen thousand and twenty thousand alligators in 1982. The hunters sold the hides themselves. Each hide that is sold must have a tag on it to prove it was bought according to the law.

Farms and ranches

Alligators are raised on farms or ranches in some southern states.

On alligator farms, the animals are mated and eggs are hatched. It takes about four years to grow an alligator large enough to sell. A well-run farm may have as many as 3,500 alligators. Only the adults are sold for their hides.

Some farms don't raise alligators just for their hides. They also sell tickets to tourists who want to see alligators.

People are testing another way to raise alligators. They run alligator ranches. Adult alligators are not mated on the ranches. Instead, alligator eggs and hatchlings are taken from the wild. The hatchlings are raised on the ranch. When they become adults, they are killed for their skins and meat.

Strict laws rule how the ranches and farms are run. They must be kept clean and the animals must be well cared for.

Looking for answers

There are many things scientists still don't know about alligators. When alligators are attacked or are fighting, they give off an odor. The glands, where the odor comes from, are under the jaw and also, near the vent through which their wastes pass. Both males and females have them. Scientists don't know why the alligator gives off the odor nor what it tells other alligators.

There are other unanswered questions, too. Why do some females protect their nests, while others do not? Why are young alligators protected sometimes, and eaten at other times by adult alligators? Why do some alligators attack people?

Scientists study both wild and captive alligators to learn the answers to these and other questions. They watch how alligators act. They put tiny radio transmitters on alligators to find out where they go. They put tags on hatchlings to see what happens to them. Dead alligators are cut open so scientists can tell what they ate while alive. Thermometers are put in nests to measure how hot and cold they get.

Scientists hope their studies will tell them more about how alligators live, and why they do what they do.

These alligators are on display at Gatorland Zoo in Kissimee, Florida.

What's in
the future?

As alligators continue to increase, hunters may be allowed to kill more of them for their hides and meat. As long as the killing of alligators and the selling of their hides is controlled, most experts believe that the reptile will continue to thrive. So, with careful controls, the alligator should be around for several thousand more years.

MAP:

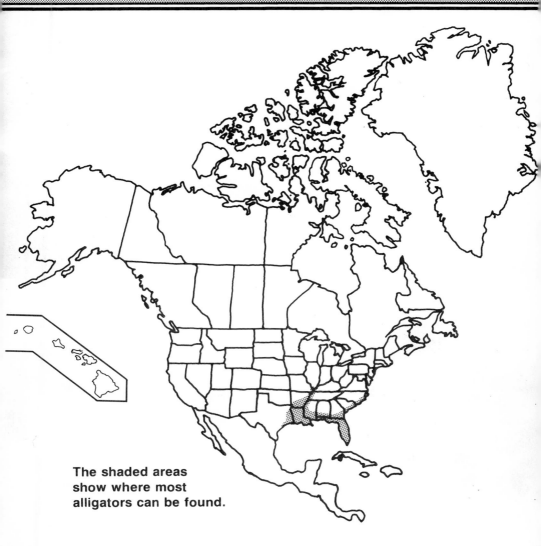

The shaded areas
show where most
alligators can be found.

INDEX/GLOSSARY:

AGE OF REPTILES 6

ALGAE 15

ALLIGATOR MISSISSIPIENSIS 9

ALLIGATOR ROADS 25 — *Trails through the marsh or swamp where alligators have dragged their bodies.*

ALLIGATORIDAE CAIMANS 8

AMERICAN ALLIGATOR 8

ATTACKS ON HUMANS 4, 34

BELLOW 22

BLINKERS 11

CAIMAN 8 — *A crocodilian found in Central and South America.*

CHINESE ALLIGATOR 8 —*A type of alligator found in the eastern province of China, smaller than the American alligator.*

CROCODILES 7, 16

CROCODILIANS 6 — *A group of reptiles with three families in it: crocodiles, alligators and calmans, and gharials.*

DIET 33

EGG TOOTH 29 — *A small, sharp bump on the end of a baby alligator's snout which helps the baby cut through the tough skins just inside the eggshell.*

EGGS 22, 24, 25

EL LOGARTO 4

ENDANGERED SPECIES 38

EVERGLADES 18 — *A large freshwater marsh in south Florida where alligators live.*

THE EVERGLADES NATIONAL PARK 18

EYES 4, 11

EYESHINE 4, 11 — *The red glow an alligator's eye gives off when a light shines on it at night.*

FARMS 42

FLORIDA 5, 8

FOOD 30

FUTURE 44

GASTROLITH 34 — *A hard object, like a stone or stick, which the animal swallows to help grind up it food.*

GATOR HOLE 19 — *A hole dug by alligators in swamps or marshes. The holes fill with water and protect the alligator during dry and cold spells.*

GATORLAND ZOO 14

GEORGIA 17

GHARIAL 7, 8 — *A large, fish-eating crocodilian found in India.*

46

HABITAT 17 — *The type of surroundings where an animal lives.*

HATCHLING 14, 29 — *A baby alligator.*

HUNTERS 5, 34, 36

LAWS 34, 37

LIFESPAN 14

LOUISIANA 5, 8

MATING 18, 22

MESOZOIC ERA 6

NEST 23

NUISANCE ALLIGATORS 40

OKEFENOKEE 17 — *A swamp on the Georgia-Florida border where alligators live.*

OKEFENOKEE NATIONAL WILDLIFE REFUGE 17

PEAT 17

POACHER 37 — *A hunter who kills animals illegally.*

PREDATORS 25 — *Feeding upon other animals.*

RANCHES 42

RANGE 5, 8

SCIENTISTS 43

SIZE 6, 14

SKIN 5, 11

TEETH 12

VENT 14 — *A hole in the alligator's underside, through which wastes exit.*

WILDLIFE
HABITS & HABITAT

READ AND ENJOY THE SERIES:

THE **WHITETAIL** • THE **PHEASANT**

THE **BALD EAGLE** • THE **WOLVES**

THE **SQUIRRELS** • THE **BEAVER**

THE **GRIZZLY** • THE **MALLARD**

THE **RACCOON** • THE **WILD CATS**

THE **RATTLESNAKE** • THE **SHEEP**

THE **ALLIGATOR** • THE **CARIBOU**

THE **CANADA GOOSE** • THE **FOXES**